A ROOKIE READER ®

WHO IS COMING?

By Patricia C. McKissack

Illustrations by Clovis Martin

Prepared under the direction of Robert Hillerich, Ph.D.

CHILDRENS PRESS ®

CHICAGO

Library of Congress Cataloging in Publication Data

McKissack, Pat, 1944-
  Who is coming?

  (A Rookie Reader)
  Summary: A little African monkey runs away from all
the dangerous animals except one.
  [1. Monkeys—Fiction. 2. Animals—Fiction.
3. Africa—Fiction]
I. Clovis Martin. II. Title. III. Series.
PZ7.M47893Wg   1986   [E]   86-11805
ISBN 0-516-02073-0

Little Monkey lives in Africa.

Run, Little Monkey, run!
Who is coming?

Crocodile is coming.
Run!

Little Monkey ran up.

Run, Little Monkey, run!
Who is coming?

8

Snake is coming.
Run!

Little Monkey ran down.

Run, Little Monkey, run!
Who is coming?

Leopard is coming.
Run!

Little Monkey ran over.

Run, Little Monkey, run!
Who is coming?

Lion is coming.
Run!

Little Monkey ran under.

Run, Little Monkey, run!
Who is coming?

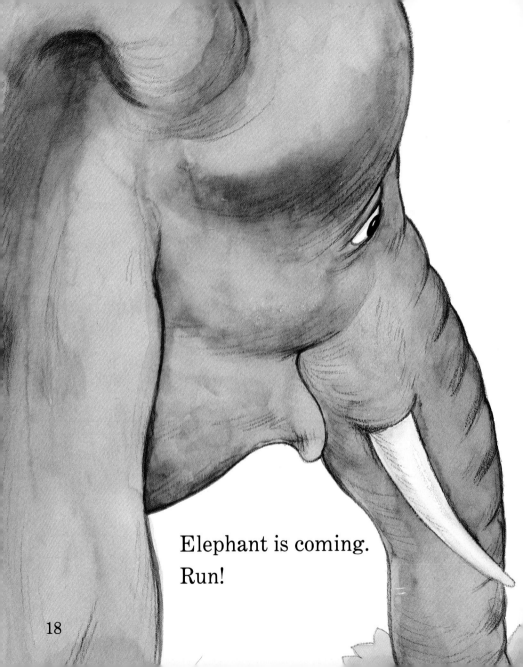

Elephant is coming.
Run!

Little Monkey ran in.

Run, Little Monkey, run!
Who is coming?

Hippopotamus is coming.
Run!

Little Monkey ran out.

Run, Little Monkey, run!
Who is coming?

Tiger is coming.

27

Little Monkey did not run.
Why?

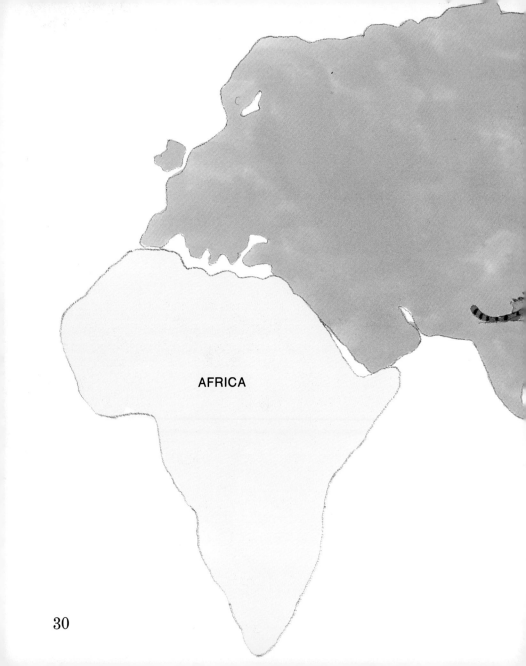

AFRICA

ASIA

There are no tigers in Africa.

WORD LIST

Africa	hippopotamus	Monkey	snake
are	in	no	there
coming	is	not	tiger(s)
crocodile	leopard	out	under
did	lion	over	up
down	little	ran	who
elephant	lives	run	why

About the Author

Patricia C. McKissack is the president of All-Writing Services, a company that provides free-lance writing, editing, and teaching of writing to various businesses, industry, and educational facilities. Mrs. McKissack teaches a writing course at the University of Missouri-St. Louis, and conducts communication workshops throughout the country. She wrote and performed *L Is For Listening*, a pre-school radio program designed to teach listening skills, for KWMU Radio Station in St. Louis. Mrs. McKissack has a Masters Degree in Early Childhood Literature, and has written several books for children and adults. St. Louis is her home, where she enjoys gardening and growing roses with her husband and three children.

About the Artist

Clovis Martin is a graduate of the Cleveland Institute of Art. During a varied career he has art directed, designed and illustrated a variety of reading, educational, and other products for children. He resides with his wife and daughter in Cleveland Heights, Ohio.